Flowers Are Almost Forever

by

LIBBEY OLIVER

D1115187

Brandylane Publishers, Inc.

White Stone, Virginia

❋ Brandylane Publishers, Inc.

P.O. Box 261, White Stone, Virginia 22578
(804) 435-6900 or 1 800 553-6922
e-mail: brandy@crosslink.net

ON THE COVER:

The Flower Girl by Epps Perrow
    An original watercolor owned by the author, it
    was painted in 1941 in Charleston, South Carolina. Epps
    Perrow lives and paints in Hurt, Virginia, outside Lynchburg.

Library of Congress Cataloging-in-Publication Data

Oliver, Libbey Hodges.
    Flowers are almost forever / by Libbey Oliver.
        p.   cm.
    1. Flower arrangement. 2. Cut flowers. I. Title.
SB449.052 1999   745.92'2—dc21   99-16969
                                                            CIP

ISBN 1-883911-35-4

Acknowledgments

*T*he genesis for this book came from Gale Roberts and Peg Smith with whom I presented a program for our garden club. I am grateful for their knowledge and insights in the care and handling of cut flowers. They reignited my longtime interest in this constantly evolving subject.

A number of individuals provided professional and technical advice, including:

- Dr. Jim DelPrince, Mississippi State University
- Norah T. Hunter, Brigham Young University, author of *The Art of Floral Design*
- Terresa P. Lanker, Ohio State University
- William J. McKinley Jr., Kishwaukee College, author of *The Cut Flower Companion*
- Holly Money-Collins, City College of San Francisco
- Dr. H. Paul Rasmussen, Utah State University
- Dr. Michael Reid, University of California, Davis
- Dr. Arthur O. Tucker, Delaware State University
- Dr. Stewart Ware, College of William and Mary

- Dr. James W. Boodley, manager, horticultural research and project development, Smithers-Oasis
- Jim Daly, vice president of operations, Floralife
- Jim Krone, executive vice president, Roses Inc.

- Barbara Lenhard, Floral Marketing Assn.
- Jim Morley, vice president, American Floral Services, Inc.
- Darren Russell, brand business manager, Smithers-Oasis
- Kay Ruth, president, Vita Products
- Richard Salvaggio, vice president of floral publications for Teleflora
- W. Kurt Schroeder, vice president of sales and marketing, Floralife
- Dr. Pawan Srivastava, Syndicate Sales, Inc.
- Shelley Urban, managing editor, *Florists' Review*
- René van Rems, director of promotion, California Cut Flower Commission

- Louise Bennett, Rosebank Farms, John's Island, South Carolina
- Robert Ciucci, Century Supply and Cut Flower Co.
- Robbie East, Fields of Flowers, Purcellville, Virginia
- Becky Heath, Brent and Becky's Bulbs, Gloucester, Virginia
- Patricia Hicks, Petals from Patricia, North, Virginia
- Wayne Jones, Flowers—Wayne Jones, Virginia Beach, Virginia
- Terry Mayberry, The Roy Houff Co.
- Edwin Van deBovenkamp, Castle Hayne Farms, Wilmington, North Carolina

Among amateur authorities in their societies from whom I sought advice were Russell Anger, Howard Jones, and Jack Rascoe, rosarians; Betty Hotchkiss, a camellia exhibitor; and Naomi Liggett, a daffodil exhibitor.

Special thanks to flower arranging and gardening friends Jewell Lynn Delaune, Marguerite Moncure Lamond,

Lucile MacLennon, Mary Anne Cesario, Cynthia Zeigler-Bernstein, Helen Waldron, and Nancy Hugo.

I wish to thank my editor, Joanne Foster, for her professional advice in bringing my book into focus. I am also grateful for the editorial expertise of Susan Bruno and the artistic abilities of Kem Putney with The Williamsburg Wordsmith.

I appreciate Bettye Pope's love of flowers that came through in her skilled drawings that illustrate this book.

Finally, a special thank-you to my husband, Alex, who is so good at pointing me in the right direction and sending me a little further than I would have gone on my own.

TABLE OF CONTENTS

INTRODUCTION

I am happiest when working with flowers, either in the ground or in arrangements. No one can avoid smiling when looking at a pretty flower.

A well-grown or cared for flower can stand on its own without a fancy design. Once cut, a flower has special requirements, just as it did when in the garden. This book will provide techniques to keep the cut flowers you buy or grow looking their best for as long as possible in your home.

The care and handling of cut flowers involves more than just one or two steps beyond conditioning. The flower requires proper treatments and surroundings every step of the way. Charles Masson, who ran La Grenouille, the New York restaurant famed for its flowers and food, said, " . . . each person has a different approach with flowers. The more one deals with flowers, the more personal it becomes." The person who works with flowers can make very good use of the latest scientific research, but she also needs to have a commonsense view of how a flower will react in a given environment, just as a good cook or potter knows that after a point, she senses the right way to handle the ingredients or clay based on facts.

I was fortunate to absorb the essence of flower arranging from my mother; from Edna Pennell, my predecessor at Colonial Williamsburg; and from Sheila Macqueen, my favorite English flower arranger. Each shared with me a passionate love for flowers. If you have cared for the flowers you use, your arrangements will reflect your style and personality. The flowers will be fresh and natural; they will not need wiring, nor will they embarrass you by drooping when you turn your back.

Violets that I picked and made into corsages for Easter as a child taught me my first cut flower lesson. I learned that I had to gather them before everyone else rose (the Easter rabbit was always ahead of me). Of course, it was cool, if not chilly, and the violets were full of water before I placed them in containers to drink even more.

As I continued to experiment with other flowers and at other seasons, I realized that I always had to collect my flowers early in the day and give them time before I attempted to "arrange" them. My mother shared her frogs, pansy vase with its pierced holes, and her bud vases. We did not have floral foam, unless an arrangement came from the florist. The arrangements—today, I would more likely call them nosegays—lasted for days as the centerpieces for our kitchen table.

One reason we enjoy flowers is that they change from buds to full-blown blossoms. They are never static. The time of this transition varies from flower to flower. We cannot expect the same longevity from an iris as we do from an anthurium. However, new varieties of iris can last up to two weeks. Most of the flowers we buy commercially are expected to last from three to ten days after surviving the rigors of transportation. I do not expect that of my wild columbine. It must be in water every moment, and it will drop petals every day.

My interest in the care of cut flowers began shortly after I began to work with Colonial Williamsburg. My work included not only a cutting garden of wildflowers, herbs, annuals, perennials, and shrubs familiar to the colonists. It also required the use of flowers from all over the world for the many special events that the Foundation hosts each year. What fun to arrange with godetia, lisianthus, or red ginger— all new to me then. I had a lot to learn about how to handle these flowers that grew in someone else's garden, in another part of the world.

Every year we enjoy new flowers becoming available on the market, and we are able to get seeds of old-fashioned flowers that have been out of style. I hope each person who reads this book will join me in experimenting with the care and handling techniques and looking for new products that aid our efforts to have flowers that last almost forever.

Prepare Flowers for Longevity

*E*veryone uses the term "conditioning" when referring to the preparation of flowers for arranging. It is the most important stage of several in the care and handling of cut flowers.

Care and handling is the umbrella phrase used in the florist trade to describe the techniques that prolong the life of flowers from the time they are cut until the time when they reach you, are arranged, and finally thrown out. Along the way, the flowers are preconditioned, conditioned, hardened, and maintained.

If this sounds terribly laborious and complicated, fear not. It is simply a series of steps taken to ensure that the flowers you handle are as alive and attractive as possible.

Actually, the growers say that they begin to prepare the flowers before they are picked. Imagine all of the steps for extending the life of a flower as links in the "Chain of Life" for that particular flower.

Most of your success depends on how you treat the flowers the first few hours after you receive or pick them. This is the most critical time in the Chain of Life. With good care and proper handling, many of your flowers may live with you for up to ten days or longer.

WHY DO FLOWERS WILT?

Insects work hard to kill flowers on the plant, whereas we shorten the lives of our flowers with our forgetfulness once they are cut. When an insect pollinates a flower, it has helped the flower achieve its goal: to attract a pollinator. The flower then withers or drops its petals, ready to leave the scene, turning the job of reproduction over to the forming seed.

How long do your flowers sit out of water while you look for a vase or answer the phone? When you receive an arrangement, do you check to see if it needs water? When you empty a bucket in which you conditioned flowers, do you wash it out? How you respond to these questions will actually affect the longevity of your cut flowers. Most people are surprised to learn how easy it is to plug the stem of a cut flower and terminate its source of water. Let the flower dry out, form a callus, fill with bacteria and/or air bubbles, and you have unwittingly stopped the flow of water into it.

Exposure to ethylene gas, a plant hormone that occurs naturally (but is also emitted from old flowers, fruit, and

bacteria in dirty buckets), will cause some flowers to wilt. It also will put carnations to "sleep," and can cause leaf drop and yellowing in others. The list of flowers that are sensitive to ethylene gas is surprisingly long. Fortunately, these flowers have been identified and processes developed to control the problem before most commercially grown flowers reach the florist's shop.

High temperatures also are a problem, for they increase flower sensitivity to ethylene. As an added whammy, the higher the temperature, the faster flowers use up their food supply. Place your plant near a window or heat duct, and then see how quickly it wilts. Flowers prefer cool temperatures and high humidity. They continue to lose water through their leaves after they are cut. Heat and dry air speed up the process, so that more water is lost from the flower than it can take in.

Flowers also wilt readily if they are of inferior quality, delayed in shipping, purchased beyond their peak of freshness, or out of season. Flowers wilt if their genetics have not prepared them to perform as cut stems, or they did not receive proper care and handling before they reached you. It's a wonder they last any time at all!

In addition, you can avoid wilted flowers and bent-neck roses by considering water and cleanliness every step of the way.

CUTTING STEMS

How will you cut your stems? For most flowers, you will need a sharp knife or bypass clippers. Bypass clippers (see top illustration on page 4), also known as pruning shears, are available at most nurseries, garden shops, or hardware stores with garden supplies, as well as through garden catalogs. Bypass clippers have two blades that are very efficient; your pruning clippers (see bottom illustration on page 4) with a flat anvil on one side or your old kitchen scissors will only crush or pinch the stems of the flowers you cut. A knife is great for cutting because it, like the bypass clippers, can be sharpened easily. With practice, a knife will speed up the job. Brightly colored clippers, however, are easier to keep track of in the garden than a knife.

Contrary to popular belief, an angle cut will neither open up more water-absorbing vessels in the stem nor speed up the water-moving process, but it does work as well as— or better than—a flat cut. Neither type of cut is likely to adhere to the bottom of a bucket (sometimes given as a reason for the angle cut), because few of us can cut that evenly. An advantage to the angle cut is the ease of insertion into floral mechanics, especially into floral foam. The flat cut stem can compact the foam as it is pushed down onto the foam, whereas the angle cut stem slides onto the foam for "grip strength." According to René van Rems of the California Cut Flower Commission, this contact assists the stem to siphon water. If you use a knife, you will find that an angle cut comes naturally.

Smashing stems is no longer recognized as a means of opening stem vessels. English arranger Violet Stevenson says in her book, *Creative Flower Arranging*: "You may even buy flowers which have been treated this way. If so, cut off the smashed portion . . . smashing helps the stem draw up water quickly, it has one great drawback . . ." Stevenson goes on to describe how the damaged tissue rapidly breaks down to attract bacteria.

Flower stems must be cut when you receive them, every two days if not used, again when arranged, and as a last resort to revive a wilted stem. Each time you cut, you reopen the stem, removing clogged vessels to keep water moving up the stem. True, the stem will become shorter as you cut and recut.

Roses and gerbera daisies are prone to take in air if cut out of water. All stems cut under water have a better chance of taking in water before air enters to fill and block the stem's vessels. Another benefit is that a water droplet attaches to the cut stem end, allowing you time to transfer the stem to a bucket or vase.

METHOD • Depending on the number of stems to be cut, cut them under a running faucet or cut them in a wide, open pan or bowl of water. Make sure that you can see what you are doing—or risk cutting yourself.

Sheila Macqueen, noted English flower arranger and

author, observed that Dutch growers at
the 1967 Chelsea Flower Show cut *all*
their stems underwater.

In fact, cutting stems underwater
is so important that commercial han-
dlers of flowers use large guillotine-type
cutters in troughs of water to assure that
their flowers get this treatment. Small
gadgets marketed for cutting roses underwater at home are available in many
garden catalogs.

THE FOUR STAGES OF FLOWER
PREPARATION

PRECONDITION • These are the
treatments growers use when they har-
vest flowers for the commercial market for optimum color,
bloom, and fragrance. This stage prepares the flowers for
travel, cooling them and keeping them in water as long as
possible. Also included might be treatments for ethylene
sensitive flowers and the use of hydrators to move water up
the stems quickly. When you buy cut flowers, you should
ask your florist about these pretreatments to be certain that
you are buying the best quality flowers.

Hydrators are becoming more popular with the home
flower arranger. Floralife Quick Dip acts as a stem disinfectant. Other hydration solutions such as Floralife Hydraflor/
100 and Vita Flora Pre-treatment are used in the trade to increase water uptake. Most florists use them with roses and
gerbera daisies to prevent bent necks. These require a half
hour or more of preparation time, whereas Quick Dip requires you only to insert the stem in it to a depth of 2 inches
for a single second. If you recut the stem, however, plan to
redip it.

Jim Morley, a vice president with American Floral Services, recommends Floralife Hydraflor/100 for use with cut stems that are hard to hydrate such as bamboo, Japanese maple, hydrangea, clematis, and hollyhock. Morley acknowledges that Quick Dip works, but Hydraflor works better.

CONDITION • This is the preparation of the flowers you cut from your garden or receive from a florist. This is the first one or two hours cut flowers spend in water, with or without floral food. The usually recommended "room temperature" for conditioning is not an advantage, according to Dr. Michael Reid of the University of California at Davis. Based on the results of his research published in 1999, he states "that re-hydration is faster at cool temperatures."

Conditioning begins with the removal of leaves that will be beneath the water as well as any unnecessary foliage. This is the time to check for pests and discard old or damaged stems. Next, cut the stem to remove 1/2 inch to 1 inch of dried out, sealed or air-blocked, and dirty ends. Then, as quickly as possible, immerse the stem in water to a depth of one-third of its length. These three steps are the bare necessities required to produce flowers that will survive.

However, for the longest life possible for open blossoms and to encourage buds to continue to open, consider these additional steps.

Disinfectants—Bucket Cleansers

Buckets and all other containers and mechanics must be cleaned thoroughly after each use. Bleach and soap, together with sturdy brushes, are the old standbys for cleaning buckets. But neither of these cleansers is formulated for the job like the new products now available. A bonus is that they have a longer-lasting effect. And these new cleaning solutions do not remove color from your clothes. Cleansing products on the market today include D.C.D., a Floralife product, and Fresh-n-Clean, a Syndicate product.

Tips for achieving cleaner buckets and vases:

- Clean plastic or other nonmetallic buckets on the outside as well as on the inside.
- Spray with cleanser and rinse once, to leave a protective residue.
- Wash any container in your dishwasher that will fit safely.
- Allow buckets to dry thoroughly before stacking to prevent them from sticking together.
- Keep a collection of scrub brushes in a variety of shapes and sizes.
- Clean glass with denture cleaner, vinegar, or toilet bowl cleanser.

If you pick your own flowers at their optimum stage of maturity and use all of the rules and hints for care and handling listed so far, your flowers will live a longer, more beautiful life—with or without floral food.

Floral Food—Preservatives

Floral food, usually sold as "floral preservative," should be considered an important tool for assisting flowers in obtaining their full potential vase life. Use it to give a boost to flowers that were cut several days before they reached your door. When you grasp its role as a sustainer of flowers, you will think that it is indispensable. In the absence of floral food, you will find yourself substituting home remedies, scrubbing buckets harder, changing water more often, and cutting stems repeatedly.

Floral food consists of a form of sugar, a biocide, a buffering agent/acid, possibly a wetting agent, and a growth regulator. Floral food comes in both powder and liquid form. It serves many purposes. Floral food adds nutrients to provide energy to open buds. It adjusts the water acidity (lowering the pH) in order to decrease bacterial growth—acidic water is absorbed more quickly by the flower. Floral food removes any minerals in the water, and prevents petal burn caused by any fluoride in the water. Clear floral food such as OASIS Clear Solution, Chrysal Clear, and Floralife Crystal Clear keeps water clear—a necessity if you are using a glass container.

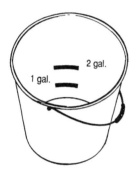

Tips on the use of floral food:

- Measure and permanently mark buckets (see illustration above) for filling with an accurate amount of water.
- Use in plastic and nonmetallic buckets, as metal will react with the chemicals in the floral food. Metal includes French galvanized buckets.
- Put a dehydrated flower in a hydration solution before placing it in a floral food solution.
- Mix thoroughly in hot water to avoid clogging stems with powdered floral food.
- Too much floral food will burn the stems by adding too many salts and removing water by reverse osmosis.
- Too little will not do the job. The product has been wasted or possibly has just fed the bacteria.
- May need more than recommended by the manufacturer or a special formula if your water is hard.

Measurements for mixing floral food with water:

For floral food:	*For water:*
5 grams = 1/2 tablespoon	16 ounces = 2 cups = 1 pint
10 grams = 1 tablespoon	32 ounces = 4 cups = 1 quart

40 grams = 4 tablespoons =
     1/4 cup
	128 ounces = 16 cups =
	     1 gallon

Water

The importance of water to flowers is emphasized by the fact that water makes up two-thirds of a plant. Without water, food cannot move up the stem to the flower; as a result, the stem will lose its turgor.

In reality, stems need only enough water to cover the cut end. However, it is wise to fill a bucket deeper than necessary—that is, at least one-third full because the flowers will use water, water will evaporate, and you need to be certain that each stem is in water.

You can slow the loss of water by removing leaves, increasing the humidity, and keeping the flowers cool; all three steps slow transpiration. Dr. H. Paul Rasmussen, director of the Utah Agricultural Experiment Station at Utah State University, conducted research on fresh roses in 1977 that proved how readily an unblocked stem can accept water. He reported in *Florists' Review* that "a molecule of water can move from the base of a 24-inch cut rose to the petals in 30 seconds, or less."

Caution: For flowers, do not use water that has been treated with water softener, as the added salts will burn the flowers.

Fluoride is seldom a problem. However, it will show up as foliage tip burn or discolored petals in flowers such as gerbera daisies and gladioli, which are especially sensitive to it.

Condition cut stems by immersing them in hot water to a depth of one-third up the cut end of the stem. In fact, for the proper handling of most flowers, a flower that is slow to revive or that begins to wilt in an arrangement should be recut and placed again in hot water.

Water temperature recommendations for conditioning range from cold or tepid all the way to hot and boiling, be-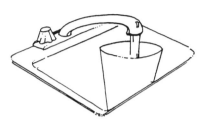cause the temperature depends on the type of flower and how urgently it needs water. For most flowers and foliages, the hot water from your tap is appropriate. This is usually 100 to 110 degrees Fahrenheit. Even spring flowers such as iris, tulips, and daffodils can handle this, although they are fine in cooler water. Hot water is a requirement for questionable flowers such as many wildflowers and herbs, as well as for roses, gerbera daisies, and tender hellebores, viburnums, and lilacs.

Hot water is absorbed quickly by a stem because it has fewer air bubbles that can block water-absorbing vessels in the stem. The flowers can be left in the bucket of hot water until it cools. The advice to use hot water has been advocated since the 1940s, when the English florist and garden writer Constance Spry consoled readers by saying, "Most of us have suffered disappointment with rosebuds brought in from flower shops . . . these flowers can be rescued. Roses in particular appreciate hot water." Until recently, many of us did not know why it worked, just that it did.

While the stems are conditioning in water, keep them at room temperature or cooler for the maximum uptake of water. Stable air temperature also prevents the stress caused by fluctuations in temperature.

Conditioning techniques that go beyond the basics

Stop sap • Nineteenth-century English garden designer Gertrude Jekyll pointed out in her book, *Flower Decoration in the House*: "Poppies and some other flowers have milky juice, which has the property of drying quickly. If they are cut and not put in water immediately, this juice dries and seals up the cut end of the stalk so that it cannot draw up water. The stalk should be freshly cut . . . the moment before it is put in the water; then the milky juice is washed away and the flowers live quite as long as any others of the time of year."

Jekyll explained very well about the sap, an often sticky, latex-like substance that seals the water-conducting vessels, the xylem. To prevent the vessels from being sealed, place the stem over a candle flame, lighter, or gas burner to evaporate the sap that is running out of it. Rubbing alcohol or a few seconds in boiling water also will stop the flow. Then, immediately place the stem in cool water. Oleander, butterfly weed, balloon flower, spurge, and poinsettia all benefit from this treatment. Some of the new varieties of poinsettia have less latex.

Condition in separate buckets • Daffodils exude sticky sap that will clog the stems of other flowers. Daffodils need to be rinsed and placed in containers alone to allow the mucilage to be washed away before arranging them with other flowers. Of course, each time that they are cut, some sap will be released. If you pull, instead of cut, the stem out of the bulb to include the white base of the stem, there will be less sap. You also will avoid the problem of the green stem splitting and curling. However, the white base does not absorb water. It should be removed from all bulb stems.

Dip in boiling water • To revive a wilted flower or to stop the flow of sap, dip a stem in boiling water for ten to thirty seconds, then plunge it into cool water. Shield the flower if there is any steam.

Submerge stems • To revive a wilted stem from plants such as hydrangea, hellebore, ferns, anthurium, lily-of-the-

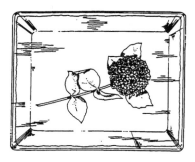

valley, or ginger, place the entire stem, leaves, and flowers into a sink or tub of cool water for twenty minutes to two hours. Use plain water with no floral food, which may spot the petals.

Some stems will need a weight added to hold them down. Standing a stem up in a tall container with water up to the neck of the flower sometimes obtains the same results because the flower head is supported and the leaves are prevented from transpiring while it takes up water. Shake or blot the petals to remove water once the stem has revived and been moved to shallow water.

This technique cannot be used with hairy stems such as lamb's ear, tightly packed flowers such as celosia, or easily spotted petals such as sweet pea.

Support stems • When conditioning wilted, weak, or heavy-headed flowers, rest them on a support so that they will harden with their heads erect. This seems to give the water a direct route to the flower. The American Floral Services suggests using a handy support that is readily available, such as a plastic laundry basket. Place the basket on its side with the bucket inside so that you can slip the stems through the lattice openings. Florists receive their gerbera daisies with cardboard or plastic supports. Ask your florist to save these for you.

Always use buckets that are the appropriate size for the stem length. Short flowers get lost in a bucket that is too tall or wide; tall flowers are easily broken when placed in short buckets.

Wrap stems • Tulips and snapdragons continue to grow after they are cut. Although their twists and turns cannot be controlled in an arrangement, they can be wrapped in damp newspaper starting about one-fourth of the way up the stem, and conditioned and hardened in tall buckets in the dark to keep them straight as long as possible. If they have already twisted, try the wrapping technique, then place them directly beneath a light. They should straighten up.

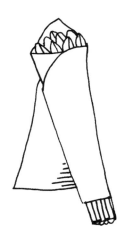

Change water • Stock, wallflowers, and ornamental cabbage—all members of the cabbage family—require that you change the water often to eliminate the cabbage odor. Marigolds tend to attract bacteria faster than most stems, so they require a change of water as well as removal of slimy stem ends every two or three days. The addition of floral food or bleach to the water will also help control the odor.

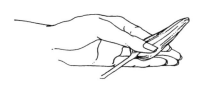

Speed bud opening • Tight buds can be coaxed open with hot water and warm humid air. This can be accomplished by misting the flowers and covering them with a plastic bag. Fat lily buds can be massaged with the warmth of the hand (if you have time) and very slowly maneuvered open from the base, never the top.

When working with a difficult flower, try this in order:

- Cut stem under water.
- Dip flower stem in boiling water.
- Submerge entire stem and flower.

- Place in bucket of floral food solution.
- Repeat as necessary.

HARDEN • "Harden" refers to the stems becoming firm and turgid. These are the final hours flowers spend in water, with or without floral food, in a cool, dark place before they are arranged. These additional eight to ten hours should be added to the conditioning time. This step is more apparent when the cut stems are placed in a cooler such as a florist uses. You can use a non–self-defrosting refrigerator. Proper hardening at a low temperature slows the metabolic processes, thus lessening water loss and the amount of nutrients expended. The result is long-lived flowers.

MAINTAIN • The care of cut stems does not end once the flowers have been arranged. You will also want to consider placing the arrangement in a room away from heat and strong light, and monitor its continued need for water. If possible, it is important to change the water in three or four days. All of this attention will ensure that the flowers last as long as possible—even if they are shorter and the arrangements become smaller.

Remember:

- Remove old flowers.
- Recut stems to revive.
- Rearrange the surviving flowers.

An arrangement that must last five to seven days with little attention other than the addition of water will benefit from having had the flowers conditioned and arranged in floral food solution.

FEED THE FLOWER, NOT THE BACTERIA

*E*nglish garden designer Gertrude Jekyll, best known for her use of color, was not timid about speaking her mind. In 1907, she cautioned in her book *Flower Decoration in the House*: "Many people advise drugs and chemicals in the water in which flowers are put." She preferred plain water, and continued by saying, "But then fresh water is cheap . . . "

The favorite tonic shared among garden clubbers today is used for reviving narcissus bulbs. The advice is to add a douse of vodka to the water in which they stand—and they will then "stand at attention."

Ever since garden clubs began, old wives' tales and remedies for caring for your cut flowers have been passed around. They have persisted because we like quick fixes and easy answers. Although there may be a grain of truth to many of the methods, proven contemporary approaches will help you eliminate guesswork and the unnecessary mess associated with these magic potions.

Your conditioning techniques will improve if you understand why these old-fashioned methods might have worked. At any rate, we all need a special ingredient in our bag of tricks to make us feel we have tried everything to prolong the life of our flowers.

PLAYING THE MAD SCIENTIST

Alcohol • Rubbing or isopropyl alcohol (70 percent denatured ethyl alcohol), vodka, gin, and 95 percent grain alcohol (still touted though no longer available on the market) will disinfect, but they can be put to better uses. If you want to try using alcohol, add 1 teaspoon to a quart of water. Suggested for use with sweet pea, salvia, lily-of-the-valley, calla lily, larkspur, baby's breath, clematis, hyacinth, and daisy.

Alum • Is aluminum sulfate, which with water forms one chemical that decreases the water pH and another that prevents bacteria from clogging the stems. Causes minerals to precipitate in water instead of clogging stems, but hydration solutions and floral food take care of this for you. Use with euphorbia.

Aspirin • Is acid and could lower the water pH, thus controlling bacteria, but it is difficult to gauge the amount needed, and additives in aspirin could be detrimental to flowers. In addition, aspirin does not dissolve easily.

Bleach • Will disinfect and clear cloudy water, but it can be toxic to stems and will stain clothes and furniture. The object (i.e., the bucket) must be cleaned, then soaked for five to ten minutes for bleach to be effective. It also evaporates rapidly, diminishing benefits as a bucket cleaner. If you wish to try using bleach, use 1/4 teaspoon to a quart of water in a vase, or 3/4 cup to a gallon for cleaning buckets.
Note: You can remove sticky sap from poinsettias by using 2 teaspoons of 10 percent chlorine bleach in a gallon

of water, made by mixing one part bleach to nine parts water.

Boric acid • Suggested for use with carnations at a ratio of 1/2 teaspoon to a quart of water.

Charcoal • Today, this is activated carbon. It filters smells and impurities out of the water and clears cloudy water just as it does in an aquarium, but do not use briquettes to do this.

Cut at an angle • Makes it easier to insert a stem into an arrangement, but it does not open up more vessels, nor can it help water to be pulled up the xylem any faster.

Deep water • Provides extra water for evaporation and transpiration, but flowers just won't use that much. You will only build your muscles by carrying unnecessarily full buckets. About one-third full is all you will need.

Lemon/lime soda • Contains citric acid that is often included in hydration solutions and carbonation that helps keep water clear. But sodas are unstable, and gauging the amount needed is often difficult. Do not use diet sodas because they lack the needed sugar. Caution: Water with soda might also attract insects. Still want to try it? Mix one part soda with two parts water; add 1/4 teaspoon of bleach per quart.

Lily stamens • Removing stamens may prevent pollination, thus slowing senility, but it must be done before pollen touches the stigma. Good idea because it will also prevent stains to clothing.

Misting • Opinions differ concerning whether it is worthwhile. Some say use only with an anti-transpirant, others only on tropicals. Still others think it may cause mold.

Mouthwash • It is usually a germicide/biocide. Precaution: Do not use any flavored mouthwash. If you choose to try the mouthwash method, mix 1 tablespoon to a gallon of water.

Oil of cloves • This contains eugenol, which controls the growth of microorganisms. Suggested for use with chrysanthemums.

Oil of peppermint • Dipping stems in 1/2 inch of the oil for about five seconds is suggested for use with iris, daisy, agapanthus, hollyhock, snapdragon, cosmos, dahlia, thermopsis, gerbera daisy, hosta, and honeysuckle.

Pennies • Once made of pure copper, even then these coins would not have made an acidic solution, but tossing a few in the vase water allows it to double as a wishing well.

Pinprick • Making this in the neck of a tulip might keep it from bending, but it cannot release air bubbles because they are lodged at the base of the stem.

Plunge up to the neck • Deep water will decrease the pull of gravity, allowing water to be pulled up the stem more easily. It will also eliminate air circulation. Stressed flowers benefit from being submerged vertically or horizontally.

Reusing floral foam • We have all done it, although we know that old foam contains bacteria and air pockets. At least rinse it, and do not allow it to dry out before reusing it. Keep the moist foam cool and in a plastic bag.

Smashing stems • Does not show immediate harm, but it creates damaged material for bacteria to feed upon. It also encourages the formation of protein to seal the wounded stem, eventually closing the xylem.

Stem splitting • A vertical cut in the base of the stem does not seem to help or hurt water absorption.

Table sugar • Sugar is a carbohydrate and a nutrient for flowers, but used alone in water it will provide food for bacteria that will plug flower stems. Never add sugar alone to water; use only if combined with bleach.

Vinegar • This will increase the acidity of the water, but it is difficult to gauge the amount needed.

Home Brews and Recipes

Stimulants

Stimulants give flowers a quick boost. If overdone, they can also end the life of the flower. Russ Anger, past chairman of the American Rose Society Arrangements Judging Committee, is a believer in commercial floral products. But he also sees stimulants as another "tool" available to arrangers.

In an article Anger wrote for the *American Rose Annual* in 1994 titled "Fixing the Water: The Use of Floral Preservatives," he sets forth several possibilities. He has not tried the use of salt, which is repeated over and over in many publications.

Salt
Mix:
   2 tablespoons salt
   1/2 cup water

Place plants in the mixture for 1 1/2 minutes, then place in water for 1 1/2 hours. Suggested to refresh aster, begonia, calla, hollyhock, rose, coreopsis, poppy, snapdragon, marigold, and poinsettia.

Gin

Quickly immerse the dry stem of maple, poppy, acacia, thistle, caladium, or gerbera daisy into straight gin.

Vinegar

Grasses, bamboo, and reeds will have a better chance of surviving if placed briefly in vinegar. Also suggested for use with ranunculus, anemone, tulip, and hosta foliage.

Petal Adhesives

Flowers such as chrysanthemums and dahlias are sometimes prone to falling apart. To prevent this, never pull off loose petals because they are all attached together. However, with adhesives you can secure these petals at the back of the head. Commercial adhesives such as Petal Proofer by Design Master and Mum Tight by Floralife may be used to lessen petal drop from the flower.

Several tips for homemade adhesives have been reproduced here with permission of Teleflora 1999 from the book *Purchasing and Handling Fresh Flowers and Foliage* printed by Redbook Florist Services in 1991.

To make a glue dip, mix one part white glue (such as Elmer's Glue-All) to three parts water. Dip flowers into this mixture to seal them and prevent shattering.

To make gelatin sealer, dissolve one envelope of unflavored gelatin in 1 cup of boiling water. Cool the mixture to room temperature, then paint it onto the backs of delicate flowers. Set them covered in the refrigerator to stiffen.

Candle wax can also be used to hold petals in place on such flowers as dahlias. Drip the wax at the base of the petal where it connects to the stem.

No More One-Night Stands

$\mathcal{N}$ ow comes the fun—arranging your fresh flowers! Do not forget that the maintenance of cut flowers that have been conditioned and hardened is an ongoing process that continues through arranging. Do not drop the last links in this vital Chain of Life.

VASES

Containers that hold flowers range from those made especially for the job, such as vases and reproduction colonial posy holders, to modern contraptions designed for flower show displays. Ideally, the vase will hold water. Check for tight seams in metal containers and for glazing inside pottery and ceramic vases. To overcome leaking and to make containers such as baskets usable, liners can be slipped inside porous and questionable receptacles. Remember: both vases and liners must be cleaned before use.

Liners come in many forms. Look in your kitchen for old butter tubs, mixing bowls, glasses, and storage containers that can be transformed into suitable liners. If a vase will be used often, it is sensible to buy and use a liner for it rather than putting wear and tear on the vase. Basket liners, plastic pot saucers, and foil bread pans make flexible liners.

WATER AND FLORAL FOOD

The ideal container in which to arrange flowers will hold enough water to last for three to five days. Add water each day to make certain all stems remain beneath the water surface. If flowers are in a clear glass vase, you will be able to watch the water level. You will observe that the most water is lost when the flowers are the freshest.

As added protection, a floral food solution can be added to the water in vases to continue to keep the stems open and supplied with nutrients. Do not guess the amounts. Measure the water and floral food according to package directions, mix, and then add to the vase. Use warm water to improve mixing.

You will want the water to remain clear when it is visible in glass. Each brand of floral food sells a special formulation to keep the water clear. As a substitute, with caution you can add a few drops of bleach into a glass vase to keep the water clear and odor free.

Tip about floral food:

- If you discard water that contains floral food outside on the same spot continuously, it will turn that soil acid.

MECHANICS

In flower arranging language, "mechanics" are the devices or supports that hold the flowers in place. Frogs, wire, floral foam, pin holders, stakes, and water tubes all come under that designation. Your vase and your style of arranging will determine which mechanics to use to support your flowers. Most flowers will do as well, if not better, when placed directly into the vase in direct contact with water, with no mechanics. This method is possible with flowers arranged in a casual bouquet in an upright vase that supports the stems. For extra support, a few stems of foliage can be arranged or a bare woody stem or two can be wedged below the water to hold the flowers in place.

Frogs and Pin Holders

Frogs and pin or needlepoint holders, known as a *kenzan* in Japanese arranging, should be your first option to hold

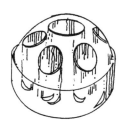

flowers. Although not so common today, they come in various shapes and sizes. Some pin holders are sold covered with a wire "cage" dome over the pins for double holding (right). Another, more flexible, style is the hairpin design sold since 1936 (bottom left).

All of these pin holders have enough weight to stay in place without being attached to the vase. Try to use the largest possible pin holder for

a particular vase. Otherwise, if it is too small and slips, you might need to use floral clay to hold it in place. Once a pin holder is attached, you will be reluctant to remove it, which will make cleaning it difficult. The Japanese also have devised a rubber ring that fits around the base of a pin holder to prevent it from moving. Even a shallow plastic lid will act as a base. The Japanese also have devised a pin cleaner and straightener "all-in-one" tool, the kenzan okoshi.

Tips to conceal mechanics or stems in glass vases:

- Camouflage a pin holder with marbles or stones. Using marbles alone to hold stems can be frustrating. They move around and are difficult to insert soft stems between.

- Attach waterproof floral tape in a grid design to the top of the vase (see illustration below). Then insert the stems through the openings. The tape, usually green, also comes in clear. This method can be used on any container to support the flowers instead of using a pin holder. The tape will only adhere to dry surfaces. Make sure your hands are dry before beginning work.
- Crush stiff cellophane around the inside of the vase to help hide stems.
- Wire netting in the top of the vase can be concealed to hold the stems.

Wire netting—chicken wire—is flexible enough to push into the top of a vase. It comes with one-inch or two-inch openings to catch stems. However, wire netting will rust, unless it is the green-coated variety that can be found in floral supply stores. The green wire is very flexible and easy to "crumble."

Wire netting can be taped to the top of any vase or crushed in layers to give support while allowing stems to be directly in water. It also can be used to reinforce floral foam for large arrangements by making a single-layer cover over the foam.

Floral Foam

Floral foam is widely available for holding flower stems and supplying water for flowers. Floral foam certainly is not new.

- Sno-pak was introduced in 1948 by Floralife to hold water and flower stems.
- OASIS was introduced in 1954 by Smithers Laboratories as "molded water."

Tips for using floral foam:

- Use the density of foam best suited for the stems and scale of your arrangement. Check brands for adjectives such as "springtime" or "finesse" for soft stems, "regular" and "standard" for most arrangements, or "deluxe" for heavy, woody stems.
- Blocks that are punched (have dots) absorb water faster. They have "instant" in the name.
- Use the shape that conforms to your design. Foam comes in wreath shapes, as O'DAPTER holders, IGLU holders, cylinders, cages, and extra large blocks. It also is available wrapped in plastic as a RAQUETTES holder.
- Do not arrange in dry foam. Always soak the foam first.
- Soak in floral food solution.
- Most blocks hold two quarts of water or solution.
- Do not force a block into water. Allow it to float and sink naturally.
- Soak with punched side down. Any words will then be on top.
- Do not continue to reuse soaking water; byproducts drain into it.
- Do not soak more than twenty-four hours prior to use. The structure breaks down and bacteria begin to grow.
- Push soaked foam securely into vase. Saturated foam will not float or move. Anchor with

waterproof floral tape only if the design is to be top heavy in a low or lightweight container.

- Leave space around the foam—cut a channel if necessary—to add water in the vase.
- Keep a reservoir of water around the foam because it is not a substitute for water.
- For best results, do not extend foam more than 3/4 inch above the edge of the vase. The further it extends out of the water, the harder it is for water to be drawn up.
- Round edges of the floral foam for easier insertion of stems.
- Insert stems at least 1/2 inch into foam in order for stems to obtain the best water absorption.
- Do not pull a stem partially out. Remove and reinsert fully to keep the base of the stem in touch with the water.
- Hold stem close to its base to prevent from bending when inserting.

Florist's Picks and Hyacinth or Bulb Stakes

Both picks and stakes are green wood, and are the diameter of a pencil. The florist's picks have wire attached and are available in 2 1/2-inch, 4-inch, and 6-inch sizes. The bulb stake is available in 12-inch height. These can be used to support weak or hollow stems, either taped beside the stem or inside of it. They also can extend a water tube to hold a short stem.

Water Tubes

A special flower that is too short to use in an arrangement can be saved. Place it in a water tube or vial, which is plastic with a rubber cap. Attach the tube to a florist's pick or bulb stake with floral tape if the tube needs an extension.

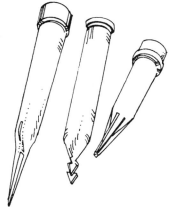

Insert the stem in the tube, after adding water with floral food and replacing the rubber top. The pick or stake can be placed wherever the stem is needed. Always condition a flower to be used in a tube. Water tubes hold just about enough water for one day.

KEEP THE ROOTS

Plants that are very short, exude sap, or wilt if picked can be dug up and, with or without a pot, placed in a plastic bag, or rinsed of any soil and placed in water. The pansy, bulbs such as the hyacinth, and leafy plants such as lettuce fall into this category. Use these plants to create a pot-et-fleur, a combination of potted plants and cut flowers. Add the plants to the garden when the arrangement is disassembled.

LOCATION OF THE ARRANGEMENT

Water vapor continues to be given off from foliage after a stem has been cut. Another source of evaporation is from the surface of the water. Dry air, drafts, sunlight, and warm temperatures (above 34 to 50 degrees Fahrenheit is warm for most flowers) increase the loss of water. However, this is real life where maintaining optimal conditions for cut flowers is not practical in anyone's home or any public space where an arrangement will be situated.

You can control the environment by avoiding a window in direct light, or a warm spot on a television, or anyplace directly over a heating duct. If possible, move your arrangement to a cooler area, such as a basement or garage, at night or when no one is around to admire it.

MAINTAIN THE ARRANGEMENT

This is the simple stage. Enjoy! However, do remember to add water and remove spent flowers from stems or entire stems, if necessary. Rather than remove an entire stem that has gone by and disturb others, sometimes it is best just to cut off the bloom. Dust away fallen petals and pollen. Watering is best accomplished with a long, narrow-necked watering can or a bulb-type turkey baster for small or narrow-necked vases. The additional water need not be hot, unless you are recutting stems that are wilted. To extend the life of the flowers, remove them in four to six days, recut, and rearrange. This probably will make the arrangement shrink in size somewhat. Most important, discard the arrangement before it gets wilted or smelly. Then remember to clean the vase or liner.

CORSAGES

Corsages and handheld bouquets will hold up out of water briefly if they get proper care and handling. Keep them in water, covered with plastic, in a refrigerator for as long as possible. Crowning Glory is an anti-transpirant made by John Henry that can be sprayed on flowers to seal in moisture. Hawaiian Floral Mist is a floral food spray that soaks into the fiber of the plant. Both must be sprayed in a very fine mist. Practice ahead of time on sensitive flowers. If the flower turns brown or spotted, spray only the back side of the bloom.

FLOWERS AS DECORATIONS ON FOOD

The obvious—but most important—point when placing flowers on or near food is only to use flowers that have not been treated or sprayed with chemicals. These should be flowers that will not cause harm if accidentally eaten. Prior to being displayed, they should be conditioned, hardened, and left in water until it is time to cut them.

SHOW OFF YOUR BLOOMS

Here are some tips from plant societies and exhibitors for handling some popular flowers: Although these methods may go beyond the everyday needs for cutting and enjoying flowers at home, the recommendations are sound and can be adapted to suit your needs. Why not practice at your garden club meeting? Soon you may be exhibiting in shows.

Camellia

- Cut in the morning after petals dry while temperature is still cool.
- Cut just above a leaf node or cut an entire stem back to the branch.
- Not necessary, but may spray on the back with a fine mist of Crowning Glory or Clear Life.
- Place in cup or water tube with floral food.
- Use immediately or can refrigerate for three or four days at 40 to 42 degrees Fahrenheit.
- Store in water tube in covered plastic container to retain moisture.
- *Camellia sasanqua* lasts no more than twelve hours.
- To transport, keep stem in water tube. Place on dry polyfill and keep flowers separated in a plastic container. Keep cool.

Rose

- Take a bucket of water to the garden.
- Cut in early morning or late afternoon.
- Cut when bud is half open.
- Cut above a five- or seven-leaflet leaf.
- Do not remove thorns above water.
- Recut the stem underwater.
- Condition in floral food; Floralife is preferred.
- Harden in dark, cool place for two hours.
- Refrigerate in non–self-defrosting refrigerator. Fill freezer with jugs of water mixed with bleach. To prevent the blower from running, do not open the refrigerator door.
- Check temperature with thermometer. It should be about 37 degrees Fahrenheit.

Daffodil

- Cut with knife or clippers as fingers may carry plant juices.
- Prevent the spread of virus by sterilizing cutting tool; dip in rubbing alcohol between each cut.
- Leave foliage on bulb.
- Cut without removing white portion of stem.
- Clean and groom immediately; remove chance of disease and bacteria.
- Cut; place in hydration solution. (If recut, place in hydration solution again.)
- Condition in floral food.
- Leave space around the flowers so they will not become distorted while hardening
- Chenille stem in stem might keep it straight.
- Can be kept for ten days in a non–self-defrosting refrigerator, at 40 to 45 degrees Fahrenheit, with a damp towel in the bottom of the refrigerator.
- Mist flowers with refrigerated distilled water.

Lily

- Cut in fat bud.
- Leave bulb with at least one-third of stem with foliage.
- Leave room in bucket for expansion as buds open.
- Condition with floral food.
- Groom—remove pollen from petals with nylon stocking or camel's hair brush.
- If not showing as a specimen, remove anthers.
- Harden in a cool place.
- Can be kept seven days in non–self-defrosting refrigerator.
- To help buds open, cover bucket with plastic that does not touch flowers.
- To force a bud to open, massage and work from the base, not from the tip.
- If transporting, wrap anthers.
- Check water regularly.

FROM HOMEGROWN POSIES TO EXOTIC BLOOMS

G athering flowers from your garden requires common sense—and a little bit of experience. As soon as you learn that you should pick larkspur while it still has buds, you will discover just the reverse is true for yarrow. Yarrow will do better if left until firm, which comes as the flower matures.

For best results, garden flowers need to be in good health and well watered the day before they are cut. Your responsibilities as you pick include using clean, sharp tools for cutting, and removing excess foliage before placing stems in hot water. As soon as possible, cut stems under water and, of course, allow time for flowers to become turgid. In order to meet the special needs of some garden-grown flowers, you should refer to Chapter 1. For example, a few that will need to be dipped in boiling water for thirty seconds and/or submerged in water include hydrangea, cardinal flower, hollyhock, hellebore, and balloon flower.

Along with the perennials and annuals that are the usual cut flowers, many shrubs combine handsome foliage with flowers to make good cut material. Examples of these are weigela, daphne, and kerria.

PREPARATION FOR CUTTING

You can turn flower arranging from a job to a joy with a little advance preparation. Decide which flowers to cut, know when to cut them—and how to cut them.

Proper equipment

Use a knife or bypass clippers for cutting stems for arrangements. Use a separate pair of clippers for pruning.

Take a clean bucket of water—hot water, if possible—to the garden. If that is inconvenient, place your flowers in a basket. Putting them on the ground allows them to pick up debris. Keep the bucket or basket out of the sun and away from breezes, both of which remove moisture from the flowers.

Your flower buckets need to vary in size in order to accommodate various stem lengths. Garden flowers are not as straight or uniform as florist flowers. Always jiggle the stems to make sure they are all in the water, especially if one appears much taller than the others. Try not to crowd too many flowers in a single bucket, as they will use water more rapidly than you think. Also, air circulation will be poor and the blooms may get crushed or entangled. The advantage of cutting your own flowers is that you cut only the number and length you need. Remember to add a little extra to the length of each stem to allow for recutting.

Constance Spry, who opened a flower shop in Bond Street in London in the 1930s and later began The Flower School, loved her gardens. She felt that the flowers she picked looked so pleasing in her baskets that she had liners designed to hold water in them. Otherwise, Spry wrote, the gardener "brings in a lovely mixed basketful, only to find that when these are divided up and arranged in more conventional vases some of their charm has gone."

When to cut

Cut flowers in the morning, before the sun and temperature rise. Early in the morning, plants are not losing moisture as rapidly as they will when their metabolism increases.

At this time of day it is wise to watch out for the drowsy, early morning bee that might still be lurking beneath the petal of a sunflower or gaillardia. And beware: the bee might even travel indoors with you on a flower before it has had a chance to warm and wake up.

In more northern climates, the temperature might not be a restricting factor. A bonus for flowers picked at the end of the day: plants have stored food while photosynthesizing.

Most of the aster or daisy-like flowers have centers that will tell you if they are fresh. In the center, you will see rings of disk flowers; as these open and age, more and more  pollen will be visible. Pick these when the outside or ray petals are open but with the center flat and displaying a little pollen. This is very difficult to determine with black-eyed Susans, so watch as the cone grows more pronounced.

Lilies are not shy about dropping pollen when mature. You can learn to look at the anthers on the stamens to judge their stage of maturity in order to select and pick fresh lily flowers. Ideally, you will want to pick lilies just as the first anthers peek out of the petals. Once the anthers are exposed, you might remove them to prevent staining petals and clothes.

Pollination is what a flower is designed to do. Once

pollination is accomplished, the flower is ready to drop its petals and form seed. For this reason, as long as the bees are visiting your snapdragon and sweet pea, the flowers will constantly drop petals. Flowers can be encouraged to last longer by preventing pollination. This is why some new flower cultivars have been developed without stamens. They stay immature to last longer, and they do not drop pollen. Pollen-free sunflowers and lilies are now available.

Globe thistle *Echinops* is a flower that shatters once it is pollinated. In *A Garden For Cutting*, Charles Fitch suggests covering this plant with a mesh fabric to prevent pollination.

Nectar is associated with scent; both attract insects to pollinate. Once again, if these are bred out of the flower, the flower will last longer. Perhaps we will decide that it is not always so important to have flowers that last "forever," especially if it interrupts the food chain. In fact, trials to find nectar-rich flowers were set up at several British botanic gardens. Flora for Fauna, a project begun in 1994 in Great Britain by the Duchess of Hamilton, promotes growing old-fashioned flowers rich in nectar for wildlife.

Garden Flowers

This list offers tips on flower maturity as a guide to the proper stage for cutting garden flowers.

Cut the following when they have one-third of their flowers open and two-thirds of the flowers still in bud:

Asphodel	Liatris
Baptista	Monarda
Foxglove	Penstemon
Goldenrod	Pentas
Hollyhock	Red hot poker
Lantana	Statice
Larkspur	Thermopsis
Veronica	

Cut the following flowers when they are in fat bud and showing color:

Balloon flower	Nasturtium
Iris	Peony
Lily	Poppy
Lisianthus	Rose
Narcissus	Tulip

Cut the following flowers when fully open, just as their petals begin to expand:

Bachelor's button	Geum
Black-eyed Susan	Purple cone flower
Calendula	Sunflower
Coreopsis	Tithonia/Mexican sunflower
Corn cockle	Zinnia

Cut the following flowers after they have been open for two to three days and are firm:

Chrysanthemum   Marigold
Globe amaranth   Plumed celosia
        Yarrow

Cut the following flowers when the center flowers are open but the outside flowers are still in bud:

Iron weed
Joe Pye weed
Patrinia
Tansy
Woad

CUTTING

A few flowers, such as spring bulbs, can be picked by hand without damaging the bulb and foliage. Most bulbs can have their flower stems gently pulled rather than cut. However, the use of bypass clippers or a knife will remove stems on most plants, at the same time leaving a clean cut on both the parent plant and cut stem.

How you remove the flower from the plant will determine if you have a second bloom for this season, or even have a plant the next year. Novices do not realize that daffodils, tulips, lilies, and other plants with bulbs must retain at least a third of their foliage in order to make food to store in their bulbs for next year.

Flowers bought commercially often have long stems because the entire plant is harvested all at once. If you use restraint when cutting your larkspur, foxglove, butterfly weed, or coreopsis, they will branch out and have repeat blooms after the initial major bloom. On the second go-around, the flowers usually will be smaller and shorter stemmed.

Much advice is readily available for the rose grower. The point most emphasized is to cut above a five-part leaf to encourage new growth. A hydration solution is useful to the home rose grower because it will ensure that water will move quickly up the stem. This is a good treatment to be used by anyone who cuts many flowers at home.

You will find hydration solutions such as Floralife Quick Dip useful for flowers that you pick. It will help disinfect stems that have dust or mildew.

If you pick after a rainfall or early in the morning, flowers will have moisture clinging to them. Hold cut flowers upside down and gently swing a handful to dislodge the dew or raindrops. If left damp, petals will turn brown. This spotting is very visible on yellow varieties. Plumed celosia, cockscomb, coreopsis, and marigold all retain moisture to a greater extent than many other flowers, so you might want to avoid picking them until they dry out naturally.

As soon as possible, remove foliage from the lower stem of a flower. This step will prevent water from being used unnecessarily by that foliage, and prevent the foliage from going into the bucket where it would be underwater. These discarded leaves will make good compost. Other leaves to remove immediately include soft, fuzzy ones such as lamb's ear, which will siphon water.

• • • • •

Plan ahead

If you have a flower that will be past its prime in the garden when needed in eight to ten days, you can cut it now and save it for later. Planning ahead will allow you to control the maturing of the flower and will prevent insects or weather from marring it. After properly cutting and conditioning a flower at this stage, you will need to keep the temperature as low as possible. Serious flower show exhibitors use the old, non–self-defrosting refrigerators to store their specimens.

Daffodils have been held for up to ten days and won blue ribbons in competition. You might have an abundance of flowers such as peonies blooming all at once, or flowers that will be ruined by spring rain or frost. Go ahead and cut them. You cannot lose by saving them from the weather. Peonies can be held for as long as two weeks, longer if in a commercial cooler. A florist might share her cooler, if you share your garden flowers with her.

● ● ● ● ●

A growing business

To gather flowers that will create a casual, individual look, grow your own or pick them from a local grower's garden. Seeds are available for old-fashioned varieties. You will not usually see these flowers in floral shops because they do not last long enough or are not sturdy enough to be commercially picked and shipped. This might be the only way to obtain some flowers that still have fragrance and some pollen.

According to Fields of Flowers in Purcellville, Virginia, pick-your-own-flower farms are a growing business. California and several New England states have long offered cutting gardens along with roadside stands. Sonoma County, California, puts out a Farm Trails map that lists many of the flower growers in the area to visit during a designated week. Check your locality for similar spring and fall events.

Tips on cutting flowers:

- Weak stems often are the result of growing conditions that supplied too much nitrogen, low light, or hot, humid weather.
- Ants on your peonies are okay. They are there to enjoy the nectar the plants provide and to defend the flowers from other insects. Shake the cut peonies to remove ants before bringing the flowers indoors. On other plants, ants might indicate the presence of aphids that secrete honeydew—another food for ants.
- To develop a specimen flower, remove all of the buds except one on a stem to allow that bud to mature for a strong, large bloom. Dahlias, peonies, and camellias are good candidates for this treatment.
- Always wear a hat and sunscreen when picking flowers.

• • • • •

SELECTING FLORIST FLOWERS

Commercially grown flowers that arrive from fields around the world are now seen in every hometown. Everyday more beauties appear in the upscale markets of San Francisco, Boston, and New York. These novelties will find their way to the smaller markets as word spreads.

The newest trend in California is to grow the gerbera daisy and the rose hydroponically. Stems are sturdier and longer, and the flowers are larger with excellent color. With new containers and packaging, California flowers can be trucked across country while standing in water for the entire trip.

Flowers are graded according to stem length, flower quality, and bud count. The best known flower auction house is in the Dutch town of Aalsmeer. The buyers there know what their markets at home will bear. This is why you might see flowers in New York or San Francisco that look vaguely familiar but on a longer stem, in a color you have never seen, and in an unexpected season. You will want to note the price, too.

Order ahead

By ordering ahead, you can enjoy the best that your florist can obtain. Find out when the orders are scheduled. With this in mind, you can schedule to receive the freshest flowers available. Also make plans to pick up lilies as much as three to four days ahead of your other flowers in order to coax them into full bloom in time for a special event.

Remember that if you wish to request a particular color or unusual flower, it must be ordered a week before you need it so that the florist can order it from the wholesaler, who orders it from the grower or auction house.

Keep the Chain of Life going

Once you have your florist flowers home, they will need the same attention as the flowers you picked from your garden. By the time you greet them, they should have been kept at the proper temperature, treated for ethylene sensitivity if needed, cut underwater, hydrated, and provided a bucket with floral food solution. To determine if they are fresh, inspect your flowers—their petals, leaves, and the cut end—before you walk out of the flower shop.

It is important to keep in mind that these flowers were handled in mass production. Now is the time for you to baby them. Do not stop the chain of steps that has been in progress. For instance:

- Alstroemerias and euphorbias have extra leaves around the flowers that should come off.
- Roses have guard petals that can be gently peeled away. Thorns on roses are especially pesky; they can hurt the arranger and damage other flowers. The best method for removing thorns is to wear a pair of heavy rubber gloves—and rub. Do not tear them off, bacteria can enter the rose if you tear the stem when you remove a thorn.
- Gladioli have buds that need to be removed from the tips.
- Lilies, if open, have stamens that need to be removed.
- Tulips often have soil in their leaves.

In short, each flower requires special attention.

Next, recut the stems under water and place them in clean buckets with water and floral food solution. Depending on the flower, any one or a combination of extra steps will be in order at this point. Weak gerbera daisies will require hot water and support beneath their heads. Viburnums and tight bird-of-paradise will benefit from submersion in water for thirty minutes. Use floral food solution in water for stock to prevent odor, for freesia to reduce possible fluoride damage, and for protea to reduce leaf blackening. Check back to Chapter 1 for other care and handling treatments to prolong the life of the flowers that have traveled long distances.

Tips on ordering and receiving cut flowers from your florist:

- Order flowers a week ahead of delivery date needed for the event.

- If you order a bunch, generally expect ten stems, not twelve—with a few exceptions. Roses and carnations come in twenty-five stems. Miniature carnations and chrysanthemum pompoms come in nine stems.
- Check flowers for broken heads, soft buds, dropping petals, heat or cold damage, and old, yellowed foliage.
- Check flower colors in daylight.
- Take a clean bucket or buckets to the florist, or have the flowers packed with ice.
- Keep a supply of floral food on hand.
- Use any or all of the suggested treatments in Chapter 1 to condition florist flowers.

Interview your florist about the following:

- Where flowers are grown; the closest source is usually the best.
- When deliveries are scheduled.
- What treatments have been used on flowers—for ethylene, hydration, stem cutting, floral food.
- That buckets and working areas are clean.

FLOWER CHECKLIST

Specific recommendations on the most readily available and commonly grown flowers used in arrangements are highlighted in the quick reference chart that follows. Some information is new; some already has been covered in the text. A number of flowers need unique care, so pay particular attention to the comment listed beside a specific flower.

Keep in mind that the longevity of flowers depends on numerous variables. Some flowers have been grown in greenhouses, whereas others are field grown and home-grown. One is not necessarily better than the other, because freshness and growing conditions vary so widely. It also depends on the season—which varies from one part of the country to another—and WHERE they are grown, which can be literally anywhere in the world. For example, right now florists are getting wonderful flowers from Ecuador and California.

Your flowers automatically will appear fresher if you remove spent flowers. This allows buds to open and improves the overall appearance of the arrangement.

This checklist for garden and commercial flowers provides:

- A handy reference list of flowers available to pick from the garden or order from the florist.
- Flowers listed by popular name, with the

45

botanical name in italics, which sometimes is
also the popular name.

- Vase life, which is the average for that flower.
- Comments on special needs of individual
  flowers or plant families.

Note that when using this guide:

- Submerge = Entire flower and stem under water
  for twenty minutes.
- Dip in boiling water = Stem end of flower only
  for ten to thirty seconds.

Name	Ethylene Sensitive	Vase Life in Days 1 — 5 — 10	Temperature	Comments
Acacia/Mimosa Acacia	X	4	Avoid high temp	Loses water rapidly; keep heads wrapped in plastic until arranged. Arrange as soon as conditioned and hardened.
Aconite see Monkshood				
Agapanthus see Lily-of-the-Nile				
Ageratum Ageratum	X	5		
Allium see Onion, Ornamental				
Alstroemeria/Peruvian lily Alstroemeria	X	Up to 2 weeks		Remove all foliage as it will turn yellow. Avoid high fluoride in water. May cause dermatitis.
Amaranth Amaranthus hypochondriacus		10		

Name	Ethylene Sensitive	Vase Life in Days 1 — 5 — 10	Temperature	Comments
Amaryllis *Amaryllis* and *Hippeastrum*		10	Above 45°F	Support with bulb stake. Use floral food.
Anemone, Japanese *Anemone hupehensis*		3		Cut underwater. Arrange directly in water.
Anemone, Poppy *Anemone coronaria*		8		Best arranged directly in water. Heavy drinker. Closes in dark. Phototropic.
Anthurium/Flamingo flower *Anthurium*		Up to 3 weeks	Above 60°F	Submerge. Dry to prevent spotting. Bruises easily. Maintain at even temperature.
Asphodel *Asphodelus*		10		
Aster *Aster* September flower *A. ericoides* New England *A. novae-angliae* New York *A. novi-belgii*		8		'Monte Cassino' is a well-known *A. ericoides.*

Name			Notes
Aster, China *Callistephus*		9	Remove foliage. Recut often. New: 'Matsumoto,' 'Meteor,' 'Miyako,' and 'Hanna.'
Astilbe *Astilbe*	X	4	Avoid high temp — Remove all foliage. Dip in boiling water. Do not allow to dry out. Submerge. Best arranged directly in water.
Astrantia/Masterwort *Astrantia*		8	
Baby's breath *Gypsophila*	X	10	Change water often. Needs high humidity and good ventilation. Keep away from fruit. New: 'Million Stars.'
Bachelor's button/ Cornflower *Centaurea*	X	4	Do not allow to dry out. Remove side buds to use in smaller design. Will rebloom if cut.
Balloon flower *Platycodon*		4	Cut just as bud opens. Dip in boiling water. Will rebloom if cut.
Baptisia/Wild indigo *Baptisia*		8	

Name	Ethylene Sensitive	Vase Life in Days 1 — 5 —10	Temperature	Comments
Bee balm/Bergamot *Monarda*		6		
Bellflower/Canterbury bells *Campanula*	X	10		
Bells of Ireland *Moluccella*		10		Dip in boiling water. Green bract encloses flower. Geotropic.
Bird-of-paradise *Strelitzia*		10	Above 45°F	Open sheath to lift blossom out with thumb. Remove old flowers. Best with floral food. Bruises easily.
Black-eyed Susan *Rudbeckia*		9	Avoid high temp	Revive by recutting and dipping in boiling water.
Bleeding heart *Dicentra*	X	7		
Boltonia *Boltonia*		10		Arrange directly in water.

Name			Temp	Notes
Boronia *Boronia*		9		
Bouvardia *Bouvardia*	X	9	Above 45°F	Remove all foliage. Do not allow to dry out. Best with floral food and arranged directly in water.
Bridal wreath see *Spirea*				
Bupleurum Thorow-wax *Bupleurum*		10		
Butterfly bush *Buddleia*		4		Remove foliage. Dip in boiling water. Submerge.
Butterfly weed *Asclepias*	X	4		Pick when one-third of flowers are open. Dip in boiling water. Submerge. Remove spent flowers.
Calendula/Pot marigold *Calendula*	X	4		
Calla lily *Zantedeschia*	X	10		Beware of sap stains. Bruises easily. Open under water by massaging. Use floral food. Arrange in shallow water.

Name	Ethylene Sensitive	Vase Life in Days 1 — 5 —10	Temperature	Comments
Camellia *Camellia japonica* *C. sasanqua*		4 12 hours		
Campanula see Bellflower				
Candytuft *Iberis*		6		
Cardinal flower *Lobelia*		5		Dip in boiling water. Submerge.
Carnation, Standard *Dianthus*	X	Up to 2 weeks		Keep away from fruit. Buy when bud is half open.
Carnation, Miniature/Pixie *Dianthus*	X	Up to 2 weeks		Keep away from fruit. These are multibranched.
Celosia, Crested see Cockscomb				
Celosia, Plumed *Celosia plumosa*	X	5		Cut when blooms are fully open. Remove foliage.

Flower		Days	Notes
Chrysanthemum *Dendranthema*		Up to 2 weeks	Spray or pompom flower shapes: flat top/cushion, daisy, and button. Single-stem varieties: 'Cremon,' 'Fuji' or 'Spider,' 'Kellian,' and 'Rover.'
Clematis *Clematis*		3	Pick as bud begins to open. Dip in boiling water. Submerge. Avoid drafts.
Cleome see Spiderflower			
Cockscomb/Crested celosia *Celosia cristata*		8	
Columbine *Aquilegia*	X	5	Drops petals as fresh buds open. Hybrids last 2 to 3 days longer than species.
Coral bells *Heuchera*		7	
Coral honeysuckle *Lonicera*	X	5	Drops flowers as new buds open.

Name	Ethylene Sensitive	Vase Life in Days 1 — 5 — 10	Temperature	Comments
Coreopsis/Tickseed *Coreopsis*		5		Keep petals dry. Reblooms when cut.
Corn cockle *Agrostemma*		9		Reblooms when cut.
Cosmos *Cosmos*		4		Reblooms when cut.
Daffodil *Narcissus*		8		Remove white stem base. Condition alone.
Dahlia *Dahlia*		6		Lasts longest if garden grown. Dip in boiling water. Remove leaves.
Daisy, Shasta *Chrysanthemum x superbum*		7		
Daphne *Daphne*		9		
Daylily *Hemerocallis*		1		Cut just as bud is opening, with more buds on the stem.

Flower			Notes
Delphinium	X		Floral food can control petal drop.
Delphinium belladonna		6	
D. elatum hybrids		4	
Deutzia			
Deutzia		8	
Dianthus			
see Carnation			
Digitalis			
see Foxglove			
Dill	X		
Anethum		7	
Dogwood			Cut branches the size needed for design before conditioning.
Cornus		5	
Echinops			
see Globe thistle			
Epimedium/Barrenwort			
Epimedium		10	
Eremurus			
see Foxtail lily			

Name	Ethylene Sensitive	Vase Life in Days 1 — 5 —10	Temperature	Comments
Euphorbia, Ornamental *Euphorbia fulgens*		5		Remove all foliage. Dip in boiling water. May cause skin irritation.
Feverfew *Tanacetum parthenium*		10		Remove most foliage.
Flowering tobacco *Nicotiana*		9		
Forsythia *Forsythia*		10		
Foxglove *Digitalis*	X	9		Recut often.
Foxtail lily *Eremurus*	X	10		Recut often.
Freesia *Freesia*	X	9		Sensitive to fluoride.
Gaillardia/Blanketflower *Gaillardia*		7		

Name		Number	Temp	Comments
Gardenia *Gardenia*		2		Mist with Crowning Glory or water. Handle with damp hands.
Geranium *Pelargonium*		7		
Gerbera/Transvaal daisy *Gerbera*		10	Avoid high temp	Cut under water. Arrange directly in water. To revive, dip in boiling water. Submerge. Support head while reviving. Sensitive to fluoride. New: Mini-gerbera 'Germini.'
Geum/Avens *Geum*		7		Petals will drop as new buds open.
Ginger Family Red or Pink ginger *Alpinia* Butterfly ginger *Hedychium* Torch ginger *Nicolaia*		10	Above 45°F	Submerge. Best arranged directly in water. Do not allow water to sit in flowers.
Gladiola *Gladiolus* x *hortulanus* *G.* x *colvillei*	X	10 8		Remove a few green buds at tip. Remove spent flowers as upper ones open. Sensitive to fluoride. Geotropic.

Name	Ethylene Sensitive	Vase Life in Days 1 — 5 — 10	Temperature	Comments
Globe amaranth *Gomphrena*		10		Remove side blooms to use in smaller designs.
Globe thistle *Echinops*		9		Cut before fully mature. Dip in boiling water.
Glory lily *Gloriosa rothschildiana*		8		Can be ordered with long or short stems. Keep sealed in plastic cover until arranged.
Godetia/Satin flower *Godetia*	X	9		Cut under water. Heavy drinker. Closes at night.
Goldenrod *Solidago*	X	5		
Gomphrena see Globe amaranth				
Gooseneck/Loosestrife *Lysimachia*		9		
Gypsophila see Baby's breath				

Flower	Days	Temp	Notes
Heather and Heath *Calluna* and *Erica*	9		Do not allow to dry out
Heliconia *Heliconia*	10	Above 50°F	Floral food not required.
Heliotrope *Heliotropium*	6		
Hellebore *Helleborus* Christmas rose *H. niger* Lenten rose *H. orientalis* Stinking hellebore *H. foetidus*	3 to 14; depends on maturity		Dip in boiling water. Submerge. The more mature the flower, the better chance of lasting. Use floral food. Best arranged directly in water.
Hollyhock *Alcea*	4		Dip in boiling water. Pick with at least one-third of the flowers open. Remove top bud. Use floral food. Best arranged directly in water.
Hosta *Hosta*	7		Bruises easily.
Hyacinth, Dutch *Hyacinthus*	5		Remove white stem base. Condition alone. Support stem with hyacinth stake.

Name	Ethylene Sensitive	Vase Life in Days 1 — 5 — 10	Temperature	Comments
Hydrangea *Hydrangea*		3 to 14; depends on maturity		Cut when fully open. Remove foliage. Dip in boiling water. Submerge. Arrange directly in water.
Iris, Dutch *Iris hollandica*	X	7	Avoid high temp	Remove old bloom. Release second bud from sheath if evident. Never allow to dry out. 'Telstar' can last up to 14 days.
Iris		1	Avoid high temp	Cut as bud opens, with more buds showing color on the stem.
Jessamine, Carolina *Gelsemium*		4		
Jonquil see Daffodil				
Kangaroo paw *Anigozanthos*		9		Recut stems often. Do not allow to dry out.

Name				Notes
Kerria *Kerria*	6			
Lady's mantle *Alchemilla*	8	X		
Lamb's ear *Stachys byzantina*	9			Leaves will siphon water.
Larkspur *Consolida*	7	X		Reblooms when cut.
Lenten rose see *Helleborus*				
Leptospermum *Leptospermum*	10			
Leucadendron see Protea family				
Liatris/Blazing star *Liatris*	10			Change water often.
Lilac *Syringa*	6	X	Avoid high temp	Remove foliage except below flowers. Dip in boiling water. Use floral food (Chrysal for shrubs). Condition alone. Heavy drinker.

Name	Ethylene Sensitive	Vase Life in Days 1 — 5 — 10	Temperature	Comments
Lily *Lilium* Asiatic hybrids Aurelian hybrids Easter *L. longiflorum* Oriental hybrids	X	9		Remove anthers as soon as exposed (leave on for shows). Never remove more than two-thirds of stem from the plant. New: LA hybrids (bi-colors and warm colors).
Lily-of-the-Nile *Agapanthus*	X	8		Lasts well if pretreated for ethylene. Floral food assists bud opening. Recut stems often.
Lily-of-the-valley *Convallaria*		5	Avoid high temp	Pick by pulling. Remove white stem base. Submerge.
Lisianthus *Eustoma*	X	9		Dip in boiling water. Remove spent flowers as new buds open. Phototropic.
Loosestrife see Gooseneck				

Flower	Days		Notes
Love-in-a-mist *Nigella*	8		Longevity depends on where flower is grown. Change water often.
Lupine *Lupinus*	8		
Lycoris Magic lily *Lycoris squamigera* Spider lily *L. radiata*	8		
Marco Polo *Centaurea macrocephala*	9		
Marguerite daisy *Argyranthemum frutescens*	10		Will need water often.
Marigold *Tagetes*	8		Change water often. Use floral food.
Melampodium *Melampodium*	9		Remove foliage.
Monarda see Bee balm			
Monkshood/Aconite *Aconitum*	9	X	Toxic plant.

Name	Ethylene Sensitive	Vase Life in Days 1 — 5 — 10	Temperature	Comments
Montbretia or Crocosmia *Montbretia or Crocosmia*	X	9		
'Monte Cassino' see Aster				
Morning glory *Convolvulus*		3		Cut under water. Recut often, and arrange directly in water.
Narcissus see Daffodil				
Nasturtium *Tropaeolum*		3		Cut when in fat bud.
Nerine *Nerine*		10		Buy as flowers are opening.
Nicotiana see Flowering tobacco				
Nigella see Love-in-a-mist				

Name				Notes
Obedient plant *Physostegia*	X	9		
Oleander *Nerium*		5		Pick with buds. Dip in boiling water. Remove spent flowers daily. Toxic plant.
Onions, Ornamental *Allium*	X	8		Change water often.
Orchid Family *Arachnis* *Cattleya* *Cymbidium* *Dendrobium* *Oncidium* *Phalaenopsis*	X	10	Above 45°F	Cover corsages to store in refrigerator. Do not place near fruit.
Pansy *Viola*		4		Keep petals dry.
Penstemon *Penstemon*	X	10		
Pentas *Pentas*		7		

Name	Ethylene Sensitive	Vase Life in Days 1 — 5 — 10	Temperature	Comments
Peony *Paeonia*		8		Length of bloom depends on variety.
Peruvian lily see Alstoemeria				
Phlox, Garden *Phlox paniculata*	X	6		Dip in boiling water. Do not allow to dry out. New buds continue to open as old flowers drop; shake to loosen.
Pincushion protea see Protea family				
Pink, Garden *Dianthus*		4		Pick as bud opens. Place in hot water or dip in boiling water.
Poinsettia *Euphorbia pulcherrima*		8	Above 50°F	Dip in boiling water. May cause skin irritation. New: Winter Rose produces less latex, lasts longer.

Flower	Vase life		Notes
Poppy Iceland *Papaver nudicaule* Oriental *P. orientale* Shirley *P. rhoeas*	2		Pick as bud opens. Condition in hot water or dip in boiling water.
Primrose/Cowslip *Primula*	7		
Protea Family Banksia *Banksia* Dryandra *Dryandra* Leucadendron *Leucadendron* Pincushion *Leucospermum* Protea Queen *Protea magnifica* King *P. cynaroides* Mink *P. nerifolia* Sugar bush *P. repens*	At least 2 weeks	Avoid high temp	Arrange directly in water, keep in light. Use floral food. Remove leaves as they will turn black. Heads are colorful foliage and bracts. 'Safari Sunset' and 'Discolor' are common leucadendrons. Pincushion is the shortest lived of Protea family.
Purple coneflower *Echinacea*	10		
Queen Anne's lace *Ammi* (annual)	8	X	Usually sold commercially. Allow time to condition and harden.

Name	Ethylene Sensitive	Vase Life in Days 1 — 5 — 10	Temperature	Comments
Queen Anne's lace *Daucus* (biennial)		4		Usually home or roadside grown. Place in hot water.
Quince, Flowering *Chaenomeles*		10		Once cut, color fades as it ages.
Ranunculus/ Persian buttercup *Ranunculus*	X	5		
Red hot poker/Tritoma *Kniphofia*	X	9		
Rose *Rosa*	X	3 to 14; depends on variety		Cut under water. Submerge to revive. Sensitive to fluoride. Remove guard petal. Note that better smell and single petals mean a shorter life. Soak floral foam with floral food solution before arranging.

Rudbeckia
see Black-eyed Susan

				Buds must be showing color to ever open. Remove all foliage. Arrange as soon as conditioned and hardened.
Safflower *Carthamus*			5	
Salvia *Salvia*			5	
Sandersonia/Chinese-lantern lily *Sandersonia*			8	
Scabious/Pincushion flower *Scabiosa*	X		6	Recut stems often.
Scotch broom *Cytisus* and *Genista*	X		8	
Sea holly *Eryngium*			10	Remove foliage.
Sea lavender see Statice				
Sedum *Sedum*			10	

Name	Ethylene Sensitive	Vase Life in Days 1 — 5 — 10	Temperature	Comments
Shasta daisy see Daisy, Shasta				
Snapdragon *Antirrhinum*	X	8		Flowers fall when pollinated. Maintain even temperature. Needs light for good color. Geotropic.
Snowball *Viburnum opulus* 'Roseum'		4 to 14; depends on maturity		
Snowdrop *Galanthus*		4		
Snowflake *Leucojum*		9		
Solidaster x *Solidaster luteus*	X	6		
Spider flower/Cleome *Cleome*		5		Remove seed pods.

Spirea/Bridal wreath *Spirea*		5	
Spurge *Euphorbia*		Up to 2 weeks	Place in hot water or dip in boiling water.
Star-of-Bethlehem *Ornithogalum* Giant *O. arabicum* Chincherinchee *O. thysoides*	X	Up to 3 weeks	Remove top bud. Remove white stem base. Phototropic. New: *O. dubium* (orange or yellow).
Statice *Limonium* Sea lavender *L. latifolium* Statice *L. sinuatum*	X	10	Floral food will keep the water cleaner.
Stephanotis/ Madagascar jasmine *Stephanotis*	X	3	Cover and store in plastic in refrigerator. Use anti-transpirant to increase life.
Stock *Matthiola*	X	7	Remove woody stem end. Change water often. Needs air circulation. Floral food will keep the water cleaner.
Sunflower *Helianthus*		7	New: 'Viking' spray type.

Name	Ethylene Sensitive	Vase Life in Days 1 — 5 — 10	Temperature	Comments
Sweet pea *Lathyrus*	X	8		Keep petals dry.
Sweet shrub *Calycanthus*		5	Avoid high temp	Condition in hot water or dip in boiling water.
Sweet William *Dianthus barbatus*	X	8		
Tansy *Tanacetum vulgare*		10		
Thermopsis/Bush pea *Thermopsis*		9		Remove spent flowers as upper ones open. Geotropic.
Tithonia/Mexican sunflower *Tithonia*		6		Remove foliage. Handle gently.
Trachelium/Throatwort *Trachelium*	X	9		
Tuberose *Polianthus*		9	Above 45°F	Best if arranged directly in water. Use floral food. Remove top bud.

Name	Avoid high temp		Notes
Tulip *Tulipa*		6	Remove white stem base. Wrap stems in damp newspaper to keep stems straight until use. Keep cool to slow elongation. Arrange directly in water. Does not need floral food. French and Parrot tulips have long stems and last up to 10 days.
Verbena *Verbena*		9	
Veronica/Speedwell *Veronica*	X	8	Recut stem often.
Viburnum see Snowball			
Wallflower *Cheiranthus*		10	
Waxflower *Chamaelaucium*	X	10	
Weigela *Weigela*		8	

Name	Ethylene Sensitive	Vase Life in Days 1 — 5 —10	Temperature	Comments
Wisteria *Wisteria*		4		Dip in boiling water.
Yarrow *Achillea*	X	Up to 2 weeks		Pick when head is firm, mature. New: hybrids in pastel colors.
Zinnia Narrowleaf *Zinnia angustifolius* *Z. elegans*		8 5		Handle gently.

The Care and Handling of the Arranger

*A*rranging flowers usually is thought of as a happy pastime. However, it can be wearing and hazardous to the arranger unless attention is given to your hands, back, and clothing.

Tips for avoiding discomfort:

- Provide your hands with a barrier. Wear thin, disposable gloves. Use an antibacterial hand lotion.
- Wash your hands with an antibacterial or disinfectant soap after handling flowers.
- Never eat or smoke while arranging.
- Do not allow skin problems or dermatitis to escalate. See a dermatologist.
- Keep clippers sharp.
- A tetanus shot is a nearly painless precaution.
- Exercise to keep your back strong.

SAVE YOUR SKIN

Beware of the irritating saps and oils that can make you itch and look terrible. The herb rue causes a rash on many gardeners and arrangers, especially on sunny days. Alstroemeria has been known to cause severe rashes on those who are allergic to it. And the sap from euphorbias such as spurge can be irritating to many. Even tulips and Queen

Anne's lace have been known to cause skin reactions. If you have ever suspected these flowers as culprits, avoid them. Have someone else handle them for you, or try to wear gloves that can protect your skin while you work.

The most common skin problem is dry, cracked fingers, caused by overexposure to caustic bucket cleansers or moisture. When this occurs, your skin is susceptible to dermatitis.

In order to keep your hands out of irritants and water, again handle flowers only when wearing gloves. No one wants to wear them; plastic or rubber gloves are baggy and make your hands sweat. Luckily, many types are available now that can be adapted for flower arranging. Medical supply houses offer latex or vinyl gloves—with or without powder inside them—as well as special skin lotions.

Also on the market are products that form a natural protective barrier with the added advantage of hydrating the skin. This sounds amazing, but *Gloves in a Bottle*, Hand Guard, and Vita Derma Antibacterial Lotion all claim to work as antibacterial guards for up to four hours.

Some are absorbed through the skin; all form a nongreasy barrier against irritants such as alstroemeria sap, pesticides, and latex.

Flowers you arrange that come from foreign countries may have been treated with fertilizers or pesticides that irritate the skin. If you eat or smoke, you increase the risk of ingesting a chemical transferred from a flower. Keep your hands away from your eyes, nose, and mouth.

Thorns, clippers, and knives also pose potential threats for wounds and cuts. Sharp tools will help prevent tugging and loss of control when cutting stems. This is why you want to use a knife or clippers that can be sharpened. One of the easiest precautions you can take when working with water and associated bacteria is to get a tetanus shot; it will protect you for up to ten years.

SAVE YOUR BACK

The occasional flower arranger is in more danger of overloading her back than is someone who has built up a few muscles from the routine handling of buckets and arrangements. Try a little yoga, or work with hand weights. If you have a strong back and are flexible, you will be less likely to pull a muscle. You will also have a better feeling for how to use your body when lifting.

For a simple back saver, keep the water in buckets as low as possible when moving them.

Arrangements can be awkward to handle. You cannot always hold them next to your body when fitting through doors. The heavy arrangements are always the ones that need to be displayed higher or lower than is comfortable to lift or bend. Take extra precaution not to strain back muscles when moving them.

Fortunately, sensible shoes are both acceptable and helpful when working with flowers. Your back will go many more miles if supported by good shoes as you stand arranging flowers or toting arrangements into a show.

SAVE YOUR CLOTHES, TOO

Pollen on your face will wash off. Pollen on your clothes is another matter entirely.

You should remove it before it gets embedded in the cloth. But do not scrub it out; pollen plus water equals a permanent stain. A light whisking with a rough paper towel or a chenille stem can lift the pollen off successfully. Never rub! Adhesive tape or dry baking powder also can help lift pollen from clothing. Even blowing can remove a light dusting. Try to hold the fabric very taut while trying one of these remedies. The sun will bleach out any remaining spots.

SAVE YOUR TOOLS

Knifes and/or bypass clippers are the tools of a flower arranger. Keep these clean and sharp, and you can easily use the same tools for twenty years or more. A flower arranger is only as good as the tool with which she cuts. A clean cut that does not tear or pinch the stems results in long-lasting flowers.

Many gadgets to sharpen blades are available in hardware stores, garden catalogs, and garden centers that sell well-made tools. Blades on both knives and clippers can be sharpened in the same manner with a wet stone and water or oil, depending on the type of stone, and kept honed with a file shaped like a rod. Less expensive clippers made of Teflon cannot be sharpened.

Resist the temptation to use your clippers to cut wire—unless they have a notch to handle the wire. The blade will get nicks and become dulled. Although the blade may never need to be replaced, the spring will definitely wear out. On Felco clippers, both of these can be replaced.

A little oil and a fine grade of steel wool will keep the tools clean and moving with ease. To disinfect the blade, dip into a mixture of one part bleach to nine parts water; rubbing alcohol; or a solution of carbolic acid.

SAVE YOUR SANITY

No amount of conditioning and hardening will matter if your carefully tended horticultural specimen or arrangement turns over in the car or van on the way to the big event!

Florist Barry Ferguson, the author of *Living with Flow-*

ers, travels long distances with flowers from New York City to the town of Oyster Bay on Long Island. He recommends transporting them packed in boxes to prevent breakage. Ice packs or liquid ice also will keep the temperature cool during transport.

Wedging wine jugs or using old-fashioned wooden drink crates will help ensure that your specimen or arrangement arrives in good shape. Arrangements sometimes will fit into plastic crates; at other times they require special engineering, such as a six-sided wooden base (see illustration on page 78) with rubber bands and paper clips (see close-up above) to hold a vase in place. Molded Styrofoam that comes in packing crates is ideal. A shape can be cut out to hold a vase in place. Best of all are the many foam carriers manufactured for the florist or active home arranger.

AND SAVE THE ENVIRONMENT

While you are at it, a few steps can help keep the landfills from filling up—and return some biodegradable materials to the land. You can do this by composting excess foliage and plant material from aging arrangements. In addition, place your flowers in pin holders or plain water when you can, instead of using floral foam.

When shopping, look for environmentally friendly products, such as those made by Vita Products. For example, Vita Flora floral food is biodegradable and will not harm the environment.

Glossary

Alkaline • The pH measure of water in the range above 7.0.

Alkalinity • The measure of water's ability to neutralize acids; thus, its reaction to buffering agents of floral food. It describes the amount of calcium in water.

Anti-transpirant • Water-based product sprayed on foliage and flowers to seal in moisture.

Bacteria • They will shorten the life of cut flowers by giving off wastes that produce ethylene and clog a stem's water-conducting vessels.

Bent neck • A weakened flower head, seen most often in roses and gerbera daisies. Caused by lack of water moving up the stem, leading to loss of turgor. It is the result of premature harvest, genetics, or being left out of water.

Biocide • An ingredient used in floral food to increase water uptake by controlling the growth of bacteria.

Blockage • The plugging of the water-moving vessels in the stem with air bubbles, bacteria, or by sealing from drying out. It can occur in the lower one inch of the stem up to the water line.

Buffering capacity • This is the ability of the water to resist changes in pH.

Carbohydrates • These are the starches and sugars that supply nutrients for flowers, either from photosynthesis or from floral food.

Chain of Life • The Society of American Florists began this program to bring awareness of the care and handling of cut flowers to the floral industry. The aim is to ensure that the customer will receive quality flowers.

Citric acid • An ingredient used in hydration solutions and floral foods to adjust the pH of water in order to increase water uptake. It is also found in some lemon/lime sodas.

Clarifier • Floral food that keeps the water clear.

Clipper, anvil • This design has one cutting blade. It is best used for pruning woody material.

Clipper, bypass • This design has two blades. It is known as a secateur by the English and as pruning shears in tool and garden catalogs.

Conditioning • The first one to two hours flowers spend in water, with or without floral food. It includes techniques to assist water movement up the stem.

Disinfectant • This is used to control bacteria and microorganisms in order to sanitize stems, equipment, and work surfaces.

Distilled water • Purified water—it is almost as pure as deionized water. An expensive but sure method of preventing salts and impurities from affecting the conditioning of flowers.

Ethylene gas • A growth regulator given off by plants, pollution, bacteria wastes, and fruit that is needed to promote bud development, but it also causes "sleepy" carnations and leaf and petal drop in numerous flowers.

Exotics • Term given to the new, unusual flowers and foliages in the floral trade. They are not necessarily tropicals.

Floral foam • A synthetic, water-absorbent material that is pliable enough to insert stems into, yet dense enough to support them. The brand OASIS has become synonymous with floral foam.

Floral food • A solution that usually includes a nutrient, a biocide, and an acidifier; formulated to increase and prolong flower and foliage life and quality. A term used interchangeably with the term preservatives.

Florist flowers • Flowers grown for resale in this country or abroad, in greenhouses or fields, in season or out of season.

Fluoride • High levels of this chemical in water can cause tip burn, yellow leaves, and other discoloring in some flowers and leaves.

Garden flowers • Flowers typical of those grown in a home garden. Columbines and spider flowers, for example, are more fragile and short-lived than the sturdy alstroemerias and chrysanthemums of the floral trade.

Geotropic • The orientation of the plant parts as affected by gravity; causes zigzags in stems of plants blown over or curves in stems shipped or stored horizontally if they are sensitive, such as gladiola and snapdragon.

Guard petal • Outer petals that protect the bud of flowers such as roses. They are often deformed, and can be pinched off.

Hard water • Contains a high level of minerals that cause a stem to work harder to pull water up. It is often a characteristic of well water. May need a specially formulated food, or use distilled water.

Harden • The final eight to ten hours to prepare a flower for arranging. During this time, with or without floral food, the flower is in water and in a cool spot becoming turgid.

Humidity • High humidity improves bud opening and prevents flowers from losing water too rapidly. If the air is too moist and without ventilation, mold will occur.

Hyacinth stake • A wooden stake also called a bulb stake. It is handy for supporting heavy or hollow stems in arrangements as well as in potted plants.

Hydrate • To promote movement of water up a stem.

Hydration solution • Prepares a stem for rapid water uptake; useful for flowers transported out of water, with bent neck, or wilted. It acts as a disinfectant, can expand water-moving vessels, and can lower pH.

Latex • A sap contained in the laticifer cells of plants such as poinsettias. It will seal a wound.

Mechanics • The pin holders, floral foam, floral tape, and other physical means used to support flower stems in floral arrangements.

Metabolism • All processes occurring in a plant or cut stem, such as respiration.

pH • The measure of alkalinity such as found in water.

Phloem • The vessels that move food between leaves and roots.

Phototropic • The elongation of cells on the shaded side of a stem causing it to "grow" toward light. An anemone is an example.

Precondition • The first treatments flowers receive in the commercial trade to fill them with water, protect them against ethylene, and cool them for transporting.

Preservatives • A solution that usually includes a nutrient, a biocide, and an acidifier; formulated to increase and prolong flower and foliage life and quality. A term used interchangeably with the term floral food.

Recut • The removal of at least 1/2 inch to 1 inch of the stem base with sharp clippers or knife.

Respiration • The breakdown of food by plants to produce energy to stay alive.

Senescence • This is the aging process that leads to death in a plant.

Sheath • A thin membrane surrounding the stem.

Sleepy • This is the premature aging in flowers such as carnations. It is caused by ethylene and is evident as undeveloped or inward bending petals.

Stomate • This is a minute pore in the outer layer of the leaf or stem through which gases are exchanged.

Submerge • To completely cover the stem, foliage, and flower with water in order to revive a wilted flower or to condition a flower known to be difficult.

Total Dissolved Solids (TDS) • Minerals and soluble salts naturally dissolved in water.

Transpiration • The loss of water through stomates in the leaves that causes the process of pulling water up the stem.

Tropicals • Flowers such as anthurium, ginger, heliconia, or bird-of-paradise that require warm, humid surroundings.

Water softener • It replaces minerals in water with sodium that harms flowers. Do not use it in water for flowers.

Water tube • A plastic or glass vial that will hold water and one flower stem. The stem is inserted through a hole in a rubber cap.

Xylem • The vessels or tubes through which water and solutions move.

Sources of Information

PLANT SOCIETIES

These all have regional and local chapters and can put you in touch with authorities on cut flowers as well as growing. They often schedule exhibitions for the peak of their particular flower's season.

American Camellia Society
One Massee La.
Fort Valley, GA 31030
912-967-2358

American Daffodil Society
www.mc.edu/~adswww

American Rose Society
P.O. Box 30000
Shreveport, LA 71119
318-938-5402
www.ars.org

North American Lily Society, Inc.
Executive Secretary
P.O. Box 272
Owatonna, MN 55060

COMMERCIAL FLORAL ORGANIZATIONS

American Floral Services, Inc.
1-800-456-7890
e-mail: jmorley@afsnet.com

California Cut Flower Commission
useful consumer information at:
www.ccfc.org

Netherlands Flower Bulb Information Center—press office
for Dutch flower bulb industry
information on cut flowers at:
www.bulb.com/cutflwr.html

Roses Inc.—the international trade association of fresh cut
rose growers and allied trades
P.O. Box 99
Haslett, MI 48840
1-800-968-7673
www.rosesinc.org

Society of American Florists
1601 Duke St.
Alexandria, VA 22314
1-800-336-4743

GARDENING INFORMATION

American Horticultural Society
1-800-777-7931
e-mail: gardenahs@aol.com

EVENTS AND EXHIBITIONS

Events and exhibitions—all available to the public—offer opportunities to enjoy beautifully conditioned flowers in arrangements or as specimens. They provide good places to learn which flowers hold up well and to find new flowers to grow or order.

- Flower and garden shows all across the country often have a featured section for flower arrangements. The Philadelphia Flower Show is the best known in this country. Contact Pennsylvania Horticultural Society, 100 North 20th St., Philadelphia, PA 19103, 215-988-8800. www.libertynet.org/flowrsho.

- Home tours. The Garden Club of Virginia, for example, has celebrated Historic Garden Week for more than 65 years by decorating the selected homes and historic landmarks with flower arrangements. Contact Kent-Valentine House, 12 East Franklin St., Richmond, VA 23219, 804-644-7776. www.vagardenweek.org.

- Major art museums across the country stage art in bloom events. The arrangements are designed to complement or interpret pieces of art.

  Art in Bloom by Victoria Jane Ream includes photographs of arrangements in museums that hold flower exhibits. The book can be ordered by calling 1-800-330-9321.

Supplies and Suppliers

A. M. Leonard, Inc.
P.O. Box 816
Piqua, OH 45356
1-800-543-8955
>   Wide selection of clippers, blade sharpener, and
>   replacement parts.

Calyx and Corolla
1550 Bryant St., #900
San Francisco, CA 94103
1-800-877-7836
>   Flowers and supplies. Catalog.

Common Sense Innovations
Hartshorne, OK 74547
1-800-575-0703
>   Deliver-Ease floral delivery system holds and
>   transports containers ranging in size from bud vase
>   to rose vase.

Dorothy Biddle Service
348 Greeley Lake Rd.
Greeley, PA 18425
570-226-3239
www.dorothybiddle.com
>   Updated and expanded catalog of floral supplies.

Floralife Inc.
120 Tower Dr.
Burr Ridge IL 60521
1-800-323-3689
www.floralife.com

Gardener's Supply Co.
128 Intervale Rd.
Burlington, VT 05401
1-800-863-1700
    Magnetized insoles and other magnetic therapy
    supports.

Hawaiian Floral Products
5117 Birch Ln.
Annandale, VA 22003
1-877-437-6478
    Hawaiian Floral Mist

Horticultural Technologies, LLC
11402 Old Carrollton Trace
Richmond, VA 23236
1-800-877-9833
    Transporter holds and transports containers ranging
    in size from bud vase to 10-inch diameter.

John Henry Company
5800 W. Grand River Ave.
P.O. Box 17099
Lansing, MI 48906
1-800-748-0517
www.jhc.com
    Floral food, Crowning Glory, bud opener, Tote trays
    to hold and transport containers ranging in size
    from 2.5 inches to 6 inches.

KDC Enterprises
9726 Aero Dr.
San Diego, CA 92123
1-800-448-5679
> Floracubes holds and transports containers ranging in size from bud vase to 8.5-inch diameter.

Langenbach
644 Enterprise Ave.
Galesburg, IL 61401
1-800-362-1991
> Clippers and replacement parts. Catalog.

Lee Valley Tools
1-800-871-8158
> Vase brushes and *Gloves in a Bottle*. Catalog.

Lenz Floralware
14 Seagull Ln.
Howell, NJ 07731
732-730-1294
> Water retentive polymer (clear and colors) for supporting fresh flower stems in arrangements.

Marni Turkel Stonypoint Ceramic Design
2080 Llano Rd., #1B
Santa Rosa, CA 95407
1-800-995-9553
> Vases, "pin frogs," and ceramic pin covers. Catalog.

Medical supply centers.
> Gloves and medicated hand lotions.

Nowicki Enterprises
423 Tamara Ct.
Marina, CA 93933
1-800-944-2009
> Wicki Board holds and transports one vase or small bucket per board.

One To Grow On, Inc.
P.O. Box 5372
Virginia Beach, VA 23471
1-888-383-2240
> Ergonomic tools, clippers, and *Gloves in a Bottle*. Catalog.

Plastic Industries
1-800-659-9786
> base • it trivet to protect furniture from vase base.

Pokon & Chrysal USA
7977 N.W. 21st St.
Miami, FL 33126
1-800-247-9725

Restaurants
> Buckets (food supplied to restaurants often comes in large plastic buckets).

Retail florists
> Floral food, Floralife Quick Dip, floral foam, and John Henry's Crowning Glory.

Smithers-Oasis
919 Marvin Ave.
Kent, OH 44240
1-800-321-8286
www.smithersoasis.com

Stillbrook Horticultural Supplies
P.O. Box 600
Bantam, CT 06750
1-800-414-4468
> Clippers, blade sharpener, and watering cans.
> Catalog.

Vita Products, Inc.
P.O. Box 565
Chandler, AZ 85244
1-800-874-1452
www.vitaproducts.com
> Biodegradable and environmentally safe hydration
> solution, floral preservative, and antibacterial lotion.

Walter Nicke Co.
P.O. Box 433
Topsfield, MA 01983
978-887-3388
www.gardentalk.com
> 4-in-1 tool and knife sharpener; French flower bucket.
> Catalog.

Witherspoon Rose Garden Shop
P.O. Box 52489
Durham, NC 27717
1-800-643-0315
> Stem stripper, clippers, and cut flower carrier with
> three plastic containers. Catalog.

What To Take to a Flower Show

*L*et "be prepared" be your motto when exhibiting an arrangement or specimen at a flower show. With the proper supplies on hand, you can groom flowers and revive finicky performers so that they win prizes or at least receive admiring glances all through the show.

You will not be able to run home for the following:

For an arrangement:

- Vase—or perhaps take two from which to choose. And check them for leaks before you leave home.
- Pin holder or floral foam, soaked before you leave and stored in plastic
- Waterproof floral tape
- Water tubes
- Knife
- Bypass clippers
- Watering can with long neck
- Turkey baster
- Mister
- Crowning Glory or Hawaiian Floral Mist
- Yardstick or tape measure
- Paper towels
- Plastic crate—good for carrying supplies. Later, it could prove handy as a stand if you have to check an arrangement on a pedestal.

- Trash bag

For a floral specimen:

- Appropriate display bottles, unless supplied
- Floral food—in clear glass, use a floral food with a clarifier
- Containers in which to support flowers that require submerging or supporting while reviving
- Single-edge razor blade
- Small, needle-nose clippers
- Artist's camel's hair brush
- Cotton swabs

SUMMARY OF BASICS
FOR FLOWER LONGEVITY

*M*ost arrangements last about four to seven days, according to the Society of American Florists, with a caveat to the arranger "depending on the types of flowers used and the type of care they receive." Above all, prevent stress to you and your flowers: Get your flowers in water as quickly as possible and keep them there. You can lengthen the life of a cut stem by adhering to the following techniques and tips.

Keep stem vessels open and water flowing up the stem.

- Use a sharp knife or bypass clippers, *not* scissors or pruning shears.
- Cut stems under water.
- Cut—do not crush—woody stems.
- Recut stems when conditioning, arranging, or reviving.
- Use a hydration solution to open water-conducting vessels.
- Use floral food to increase water acidity.
- Keep flowers in water when arranging, not on the countertop.
- Use HOT water (100 to 110 degrees Fahrenheit) for most stems, especially those prone to bent necks.

Prevent the growth of bacteria.

- Clean all mechanics (buckets, vases, frogs, knives, etc.).
- Remove leaves that will be beneath the water.
- Use a hydration solution to disinfect stems.
- Replace water with fresh, clean water every three to four days.
- Use flower food in water for conditioning and arranging.

Keep air temperature low.

- Harden in a cool basement, garage, or non–self-defrosting refrigerator (most flowers except tropicals).
- Avoid direct sunlight and appliances that generate heat.
- Use higher temperatures to force blooms to open.

Prevent fungus growth.

- Allow for air circulation between stems in buckets.
- Do not mist flowers.

Supply nutrient source.

- Cut flowers late in the day for the most stored nutrients.
- Use a floral food in water for conditioning and arranging.

Prevent ethylene buildup.

- Discard old, diseased, or damaged flowers and foliage.
- Never leave flowers near an automobile exhaust or cigarettes.
- Do not arrange or store fruit and vegetables with flowers.
- Clean containers to prevent bacteria buildup.

Keep humidity high.

- Avoid drafts.
- Avoid hot, dry heating systems.
- Avoid open fireplaces.
- When extra humidity is needed (e.g., when forcing forsythia), cover the flower buds with a clear plastic bag.

About the Author

*L*ibbey Oliver, who lives in Williamsburg, Virginia, recently launched a new career as a consultant to the floral and horticultural industries. For nearly twenty-three years, Libbey managed floral services for the Colonial Williamsburg Foundation. During that time, she appeared on ABC's popular show "Good Morning America" to share her methods for creating colonial-style Christmas decorations. Her designs have appeared in books and numerous magazines, including *Country Home* and *Southern Living*.

Colonial Williamsburg Decorates for Christmas by Libbey, published in 1981, has sold more than 250,000 copies. It now has a companion video on which she demonstrates what she explains in the book. Libbey has also coauthored a 1999 volume, *Williamsburg Christmas*.

In 1994, The American Horticultural Society honored Libbey with the national Flower Arranger of the Year award.

Libbey holds a degree in ornamental horticulture from Virginia Polytechnic Institute and State University. She worked as a horticulturist at Callaway Gardens in Pine Mountain, Georgia, before moving to Williamsburg.